Guardian Angels

Scriptures taken from the Holy Bible, New International Version ®, NIV®, Copyright © 1973, 1978, 1984, 2011 by Biblica, Inc. ™ Used by permission of Zondervan. All rights reserved worldwide. www.zondervan.com The "NIV" and "New International Version" are trademarks registered in the United States Patent and Trademark Office by Biblica, Inc. ™

Alisa Clark

Guardian

For he will command his angels
concerning you...

For Emily and A.J.,
my little angels.
And, for little
Zach too!

When I'm afraid of the dark,

my guardian angel is at my side.

If I need help I pray.

Everyday I feel loved,

as my guardian angel watches over me.

because God's angels protect me.

I go to bat with my guardian angel.

my guardian angel is my companion.

Sometimes kids tease me,

Each night I sleep peacefully,

my guardian angel keeps me safe.

and they will lift you up in their hands,

So that you will not strike your foot
against a stone.
Mt 4:6

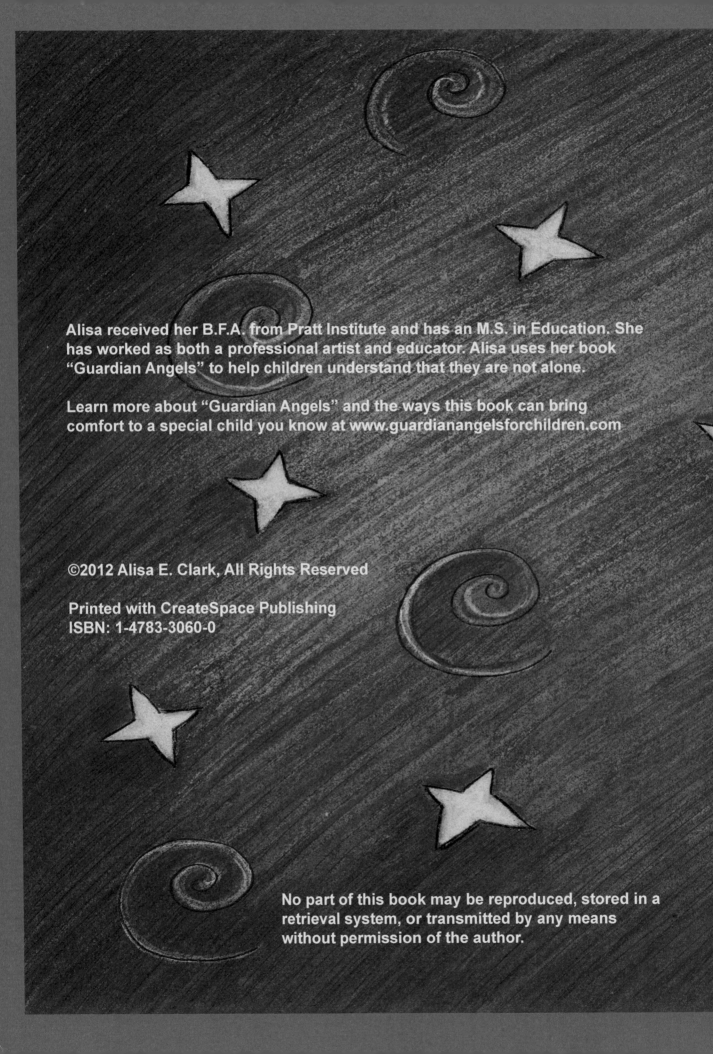

Alisa received her B.F.A. from Pratt Institute and has an M.S. in Education. She has worked as both a professional artist and educator. Alisa uses her book "Guardian Angels" to help children understand that they are not alone.

Learn more about "Guardian Angels" and the ways this book can bring comfort to a special child you know at www.guardianangelsforchildren.com

Printed with CreateSpace Publishing
ISBN: 1-4783-3060-0

Draw Your Guardian Angel Here:

Made in the USA
Lexington, KY
10 March 2018